Food

★ A very first picture book ★

The original publishers would like to thank the following children (and their parents) for appearing in this book: Karl Bolger, Francesca Brighton, Milo Clare, Jessica Davis, Daisy Edwards, Tayah Ettienne, Matthew Ferguson, Saffron George, Faye Harrison, Zoe Harrison, Erin Hoel, and Rebekah Murrell.

For a free color catalog describing Gareth Stevens Publishing's list of high-quality books and multimedia programs, call 1-800-542-2595 (USA) or 1-800-461-9120 (Canada). Gareth Stevens Publishing's Fax: (414) 225-0377.

Library of Congress Cataloging-in-Publication Data

Tuxworth, Nicola.
    Food: a very first picture book / Nicola Tuxworth.
      p. cm. — (Pictures and words)
    Includes bibliographical references and index.
    Summary: Photographs of babies and young children
serving, eating, and even preparing a variety of foods.
    ISBN 0-8368-2430-X (lib. bdg.)
    1. Food—Pictorial works—Juvenile literature. [1. Food.]
I. Title. II. Series.
TX355.T89   1999
641.3—dc21   99-19214

This North American edition first published in 1999 by
Gareth Stevens Publishing
1555 North RiverCenter Drive, Suite 201
Milwaukee, WI 53212 USA

Original edition © 1996 by Anness Publishing Limited. First published in 1996 by Lorenz Books, an imprint of Anness Publishing Inc., New York, New York. This U.S. edition © 1999 by Gareth Stevens, Inc. Additional end matter © 1999 by Gareth Stevens, Inc.

Senior editor: Sue Grabham
Editor: Sophie Warne
Photographer: Lucy Tizard
Design and typesetting: Michael Leaman Design Partnership

Printed in Mexico

1 2 3 4 5 6 7 8 9 03 02 01 00 99

PICTURES & WORDS

Food

★ A very first picture book ★

Nicola Tuxworth

Gareth Stevens Publishing
MILWAUKEE

Look,
we've been
shopping.

This basket is *really* heavy.

Mmm ...
what's this?

5

This apple
tastes good ...

... I wonder
what this
is like.

6

What's down here?

Oh, no! Here comes Mom! I'd better pick up.

Is it lunchtime yet?

8

There's
definitely
nothing in
here ...

9

... at last!
Yum, yum.

Any chance of
some more
juice?

Please
don't wash
my face.

I drink milk for breakfast ...

... and lunch

... and dinner!

Burp!

We're having a tea party.

Eat it all up,
Teddy!

Now for
a drink.

15

We're making cupcakes.
What goes in next?

16

Don't forget
the icing.

Try one,
Dad.

17

Spaghetti is
hard to eat.

Whoops!

19

We like
ice cream.

Quick,
eat it before
it melts!

This food tastes good,
and it's healthy, too!

Questions for Discussion

1. Where does the food in the grocery store come from? How does it get there from a farm? How does it get there from the ocean? How does it get there all the way from a foreign country?

2. If you had to choose between a healthy food and an unhealthy one, which would you choose? Why?

3. What is your favorite food? What other foods do you like?

4. Why is it important to eat breakfast every day? What are some healthy breakfast foods?

5. How many foods can you name in the shopping basket shown on the cover of this book?

More Books to Read

Barney and Baby Bop Go to the Grocery Store. Donna Cooner (Lyons)

First Look at Growing Food. Claire Llewellyn (Gareth Stevens)

Food and Health. Good Health Guides (series). Enid Broderick Fisher (Gareth Stevens)

The Foods We Eat. Patricia McKissack and Roberta Duyff (Many Hands Media)

My Food. Harriet Ziefert (Dorling Kindersley)

Our Food. Under the Microscope (series). John Woodward (Gareth Stevens)

Videos

Even More Preschool Power. (Concept Videos)

Food. (Coronet, The Multimedia Co.)

Food: Farm to City. (Barr Films)

Kids Can Cook! (VCA Television)

Web Sites

www.ctw.org/parents/deliciousfun/food/

mysp.com/p/eeyoresnacks/

Some web sites stay current longer than others. For further web sites, use your search engines to locate the following topics: *breakfast, cooking, food, health, nutrition,* and *recipes.*

Glossary-Index

cupcakes: small, individual baked cakes. (pp. 16-17)

definitely: sure to happen; certainly. (p. 9)

heavy: weighing a lot. (p. 5)

icing: a smooth, sweet mixture of sugar, butter, and eggs used to cover cakes and cookies; frosting. (p. 17)

lunchtime: mealtime during the middle of the day. (p. 8)

melts *(v)*: changes from a solid to a liquid by heating. (p. 21)

quick: fast; hurried. (p. 21)

spaghetti: a food made of a certain type of flour and water and shaped into long strings. (pp. 18-19)